G000067501

A Midsummer Night's Dream

William Shakespeare

Large Student Annotation Edition: Formatted with wide spacing, wide margins and extra pages for your own notes and responses.

ISBN: 9781081949884

Dramatis Personæ

THESEUS, Duke of Athens.

EGEUS, Father to Hermia.

LYSANDER, DEMETRIUS, in love with Hermia.

PHILOSTRATE, Master of the Revels to Theseus.

QUINCE, a Carpenter.

SNUG, a Joiner.

BOTTOM, a Weaver.

FLUTE, a Bellows-mender.

SNOUT, a Tinker.

STARVELING, a Tailor.

HIPPOLYTA, Queen of the Amazons, betrothed to Theseus.

HERMIA, Daughter to Egeus, in love with Lysander.

HELENA, in love with Demetrius.

OBERON, King of the Fairies.

TITANIA, Queen of the Fairies.

PUCK, or Robin Goodfellow.

PEASE-BLOSSOM, COBWEB, MOTH, MUSTARD-SEED, Fairies.

Other Fairies attending their King and Queen.

Attendants on Theseus and Hippolyta.

SCENE.—*Athens, and a Wood near it.*

motifs

ACT I

→ Site of order

SCENE I. Athens. The palace of THESEUS.

Enter THESEUS, HIPPOLYTA, PHILOSTRATE, and Attendants

→ time constraint

THESEUS

Now, fair Hippolyta, our nuptial hour

beauty + appearance ←

Draws on apace; four happy days bring in

→ Wedding in 4 days

Another moon: but, O, methinks, how slow

fertility
nocturnal
supernatral } _dreams_
chaos

forced love
appearances
can be deciving

This old moon wanes! she lingers my desires,

→ he's desperate to get married

Like to a step-dame or a dowager — _→ widower_

moon has power overdue

→ reassurance

Long withering out a young man revenue.

time is running away from her freedom

repetition of excitement quickly

HIPPOLYTA

Four days will quickly steep themselves in night;

Four nights will quickly dream away the time;

→ What she could have done

And then the moon, like to a silver bow

New-bent in heaven, shall behold the night

Of our solemnities.

Joy/control

Imagery of him bringing the city to life

THESEUS

Go, Philostrate,

People shouldn't be sad

Stir up the Athenian youth to merriments;

→ joy

Awake the pert and nimble spirit of mirth;

Save the sadness for the funerals

Turn melancholy forth to funerals;

The pale companion is not for our pomp.

Exit PHILOSTRATE

3

Hippolyta, I woo'd thee with my sword,

And won thy love, doing thee injuries;

But I will wed thee in another key,

With pomp, with triumph and with revelling.

Enter EGEUS, HERMIA, LYSANDER, and DEMETRIUS

EGEUS
Happy be Theseus, our renowned duke!

THESEUS
Thanks, good Egeus: what's the news with thee?

EGEUS
Full of vexation come I, with complaint

Against my child, my daughter Hermia.

Stand forth, Demetrius. My noble lord,

This man hath my consent to marry her.

Stand forth, Lysander: and my gracious duke,

This man hath bewitch'd the bosom of my child;

Thou, thou, Lysander, thou hast given her rhymes,

And interchanged love-tokens with my child:

Thou hast by moonlight at her window sung,

With feigning voice verses of feigning love,

And stolen the impression of her fantasy

With bracelets of thy hair, rings, gawds, conceits,

Knacks, trifles, nosegays, sweetmeats, messengers

Of strong prevailment in unharden'd youth:

Handwritten annotations:

→ fighting skills

it gives the impression that he would fight for her
↳ claming her

assertive controlling language

def annoyed fustrated emphasis

he cursed her
She's under his control

repetition of my = ownership

moon + night = dreams / rebles

he's almost comparing them

foreshadows faries

Probably associated with romance

fake

♡ = childlike not serious

his love is untrue

he made himself seem like her dream

excessive displays of love

think he's naive and stupid

4

With cunning hast thou filch'd my daughter's heart,

Turn'd her obedience, which is due to me,

To stubborn harshness: and, my gracious duke,

Be it so she; will not here before your grace

Consent to marry with Demetrius,

I beg the ancient privilege of Athens,

As she is mine, I may dispose of her:

Which shall be either to this gentleman

Or to her death, according to our law

Immediately provided in that case.

THESEUS
What say you, Hermia? be advised fair maid:

To you your father should be as a god;

One that composed your beauties, yea, and one

To whom you are but as a form in wax

By him imprinted and within his power

To leave the figure or disfigure it.

Demetrius is a worthy gentleman.

HERMIA
So is Lysander.

THESEUS
In himself he is;

But in this kind, wanting your father's voice,

The other must be held the worthier.

Handwritten annotations:

no longer feels like she loves him

→ he's supposed to be in charge

ironic ↴
It is his consent not hers

Submission ←
↳ realisation

Serious harsh threataning

→ Objectifying her
→ heirachy
Patriachal
↳ She has no control over her life

→ definitive
→ heirachy

Ownership
↑
branding

invalidating

there is no hero ↳ anyone could be it

→ moulded her

→ She will be disfigured

questioning

→ Somewhat agreeing

his opinions are more valuable

he doesn't see him → vision
the way she sees him

HERMIA
I would my father look'd but with my eyes.

Subjective

everyone has their own opinion

THESEUS
Rather your eyes must with his judgment look.

hermia has to get to know people

HERMIA
I do entreat your grace to pardon me.

appearance

I know not by what power I am made bold,

Nor how it may concern my modesty,

In such a presence here to plead my thoughts;

But I beseech your grace that I may know

The worst that may befall me in this case,

If I refuse to wed Demetrius.

just one of hardships ←

THESEUS
Either to die the death or to abjure

there is no choice where he's happy

For ever the society of men.

Therefore, fair Hermia, question your desires;

Know of your youth, examine well your blood,

Whether, if you yield not to your father's choice,

Saying she can't have children

You can endure the livery of a nun,

defeating her purpose

For aye to be in shady cloister mew'd,

empty, unfilled, boring

To live a barren sister all your life,

Chanting faint hymns to the cold fruitless moon.

Thrice-blessed they that master so their blood,

To undergo such maiden pilgrimage;

6

But earthlier happy is the rose distill'd,

Than that which withering on the virgin thorn

Grows, lives and dies in single blessedness.

HERMIA
So will I grow, so live, so die, my lord,

Ere I will my virgin patent up

Unto his lordship, whose unwished yoke

My soul consents not to give sovereignty.

THESEUS
Take time to pause; and, by the next new moon--

The sealing-day betwixt my love and me,

For everlasting bond of fellowship--

Upon that day either prepare to die

For disobedience to your father's will,

Or else to wed Demetrius, as he would;

Or on Diana's altar to protest

For aye austerity and single life.

DEMETRIUS
Relent, sweet Hermia: and, Lysander, yield

Thy crazed title to my certain right.

LYSANDER
You have her father's love, Demetrius;

Let me have Hermia's: do you marry him.

Handwritten annotations:
- in love → fertile → Queen Elizabeth ↑ not having children
- → unfitted / undesireable
- always found positive
- Is it worth it? reclaim
- → her soul is above royalty
- defiant

EGEUS

Scornful Lysander! true, he hath my love,

And what is mine my love shall render him.

And she is mine, and all my right of her

I do estate unto Demetrius.

LYSANDER

I am, my lord, as well derived as he,

As well possess'd; my love is more than his;

My fortunes every way as fairly rank'd,

If not with vantage, as Demetrius';

And, which is more than all these boasts can be,

I am beloved of beauteous Hermia:

Why should not I then prosecute my right?

Demetrius, I'll avouch it to his head,

Made love to Nedar's daughter, Helena,

And won her soul; and she, sweet lady, dotes,

Devoutly dotes, dotes in idolatry,

Upon this spotted and inconstant man.

THESEUS

I must confess that I have heard so much,

And with Demetrius thought to have spoke thereof;

But, being over-full of self-affairs,

My mind did lose it. But, Demetrius, come;

And come, Egeus; you shall go with me,

I have some private schooling for you both.

For you, fair Hermia, look you arm yourself

To fit your fancies to your father's will;

Or else the law of Athens yields you up--

Which by no means we may extenuate--

To death, or to a vow of single life.

Come, my Hippolyta: what cheer, my love?

Demetrius and Egeus, go along:

I must employ you in some business

Against our nuptial and confer with you

Of something nearly that concerns yourselves.

EGEUS
With duty and desire we follow you.

Exeunt all but LYSANDER and HERMIA

LYSANDER
How now, my love! why is your cheek so pale?

How chance the roses there do fade so fast?

HERMIA
Belike for want of rain, which I could well

Beteem them from the tempest of my eyes.

LYSANDER
Ay me! for aught that I could ever read,

Could ever hear by tale or history,

The course of true love never did run smooth;

But, either it was different in blood,--

HERMIA
O cross! too high to be enthrall'd to low.

LYSANDER
Or else misgraffed in respect of years,--

HERMIA
O spite! too old to be engaged to young.

LYSANDER
Or else it stood upon the choice of friends,--

HERMIA
O hell! to choose love by another's eyes.

LYSANDER
Or, if there were a sympathy in choice,

War, death, or sickness did lay siege to it,

Making it momentany as a sound,

Swift as a shadow, short as any dream;

Brief as the lightning in the collied night,

That, in a spleen, unfolds both heaven and earth,

And ere a man hath power to say 'Behold!'

The jaws of darkness do devour it up:

So quick bright things come to confusion.

HERMIA
If then true lovers have been ever cross'd,

It stands as an edict in destiny:

Then let us teach our trial patience,

Because it is a customary cross,

As due to love as thoughts and dreams and sighs,

Wishes and tears, poor fancy's followers.

LYSANDER
A good persuasion: therefore, hear me, Hermia.

I have a widow aunt, a dowager

Of great revenue, and she hath no child:

From Athens is her house remote seven leagues;

And she respects me as her only son.

There, gentle Hermia, may I marry thee;

And to that place the sharp Athenian law

Cannot pursue us. If thou lovest me then,

Steal forth thy father's house to-morrow night;

And in the wood, a league without the town,

Where I did meet thee once with Helena,

To do observance to a morn of May,

There will I stay for thee.

HERMIA
My good Lysander!

I swear to thee, by Cupid's strongest bow,

By his best arrow with the golden head,

By the simplicity of Venus' doves,

By that which knitteth souls and prospers loves,

And by that fire which burn'd the Carthage queen,

When the false Troyan under sail was seen,

By all the vows that ever men have broke,

In number more than ever women spoke,

In that same place thou hast appointed me,

To-morrow truly will I meet with thee.

LYSANDER
Keep promise, love. Look, here comes Helena.

Enter HELENA
HERMIA
God speed fair Helena! whither away?

HELENA
Call you me fair? that fair again unsay.

Demetrius loves your fair: O happy fair!

Your eyes are lode-stars; and your tongue's sweet air

More tuneable than lark to shepherd's ear,

When wheat is green, when hawthorn buds appear.

Sickness is catching: O, were favour so,

Yours would I catch, fair Hermia, ere I go;

My ear should catch your voice, my eye your eye,

My tongue should catch your tongue's sweet melody.

Were the world mine, Demetrius being bated,

The rest I'd give to be to you translated.

O, teach me how you look, and with what art

You sway the motion of Demetrius' heart.

HERMIA

I frown upon him, yet he loves me still.

HELENA

O that your frowns would teach my smiles such skill!

HERMIA

I give him curses, yet he gives me love.

HELENA

O that my prayers could such affection move!

HERMIA

The more I hate, the more he follows me.

HELENA

The more I love, the more he hateth me.

HERMIA

His folly, Helena, is no fault of mine.

HELENA

None, but your beauty: would that fault were mine!

HERMIA

Take comfort: he no more shall see my face;

Lysander and myself will fly this place.

Before the time I did Lysander see,

Seem'd Athens as a paradise to me:

O, then, what graces in my love do dwell,

That he hath turn'd a heaven unto a hell!

LYSANDER

Helen, to you our minds we will unfold:

To-morrow night, when Phoebe doth behold

Her silver visage in the watery glass,

Decking with liquid pearl the bladed grass,

A time that lovers' flights doth still conceal,

Through Athens' gates have we devised to steal.

HERMIA
And in the wood, where often you and I

Upon faint primrose-beds were wont to lie,

Emptying our bosoms of their counsel sweet,

There my Lysander and myself shall meet;

And thence from Athens turn away our eyes,

To seek new friends and stranger companies.

Farewell, sweet playfellow: pray thou for us;

And good luck grant thee thy Demetrius!

Keep word, Lysander: we must starve our sight

From lovers' food till morrow deep midnight.

LYSANDER
I will, my Hermia.

Exit HERMIA
Helena, adieu:

As you on him, Demetrius dote on you!

Exit
HELENA
How happy some o'er other some can be!

Through Athens I am thought as fair as she.

But what of that? Demetrius thinks not so;

He will not know what all but he do know:

And as he errs, doting on Hermia's eyes,

So I, admiring of his qualities:

Things base and vile, folding no quantity,

Love can transpose to form and dignity:

Love looks not with the eyes, but with the mind;

And therefore is wing'd Cupid painted blind:

Nor hath Love's mind of any judgement taste;

Wings and no eyes figure unheedy haste:

And therefore is Love said to be a child,

Because in choice he is so oft beguiled.

As waggish boys in game themselves forswear,

So the boy Love is perjured every where:

For ere Demetrius look'd on Hermia's eyne,

He hail'd down oaths that he was only mine;

And when this hail some heat from Hermia felt,

So he dissolved, and showers of oaths did melt.

I will go tell him of fair Hermia's flight:

Then to the wood will he to-morrow night

Pursue her; and for this intelligence

If I have thanks, it is a dear expense:

But herein mean I to enrich my pain,

To have his sight thither and back again.
Exit

SCENE II. Athens. QUINCE'S house.

Enter QUINCE, SNUG, BOTTOM, FLUTE, SNOUT, and STARVELING

QUINCE
Is all our company here?

BOTTOM
You were best to call them generally, man by man,

according to the scrip.

QUINCE
Here is the scroll of every man's name, which is

thought fit, through all Athens, to play in our

interlude before the duke and the duchess, on his

wedding-day at night.

BOTTOM
First, good Peter Quince, say what the play treats

on, then read the names of the actors, and so grow

to a point.

QUINCE
Marry, our play is, The most lamentable comedy, and

most cruel death of Pyramus and Thisby.

BOTTOM
A very good piece of work, I assure you, and a

merry. Now, good Peter Quince, call forth your

actors by the scroll. Masters, spread yourselves.

QUINCE
Answer as I call you. Nick Bottom, the weaver.

BOTTOM

Ready. Name what part I am for, and proceed.

QUINCE

You, Nick Bottom, are set down for Pyramus.

BOTTOM

What is Pyramus? a lover, or a tyrant?

QUINCE

A lover, that kills himself most gallant for love.

BOTTOM

That will ask some tears in the true performing of

it: if I do it, let the audience look to their

eyes; I will move storms, I will condole in some

measure. To the rest: yet my chief humour is for a

tyrant: I could play Ercles rarely, or a part to

tear a cat in, to make all split.

The raging rocks

And shivering shocks

Shall break the locks

Of prison gates;

And Phibbus' car

Shall shine from far

And make and mar

The foolish Fates.

This was lofty! Now name the rest of the players.

This is Ercles' vein, a tyrant's vein; a lover is

more condoling.

QUINCE
Francis Flute, the bellows-mender.

FLUTE
Here, Peter Quince.

QUINCE
Flute, you must take Thisby on you.

FLUTE
What is Thisby? a wandering knight?

QUINCE
It is the lady that Pyramus must love.

FLUTE
Nay, faith, let me not play a woman; I have a beard coming.

QUINCE
That's all one: you shall play it in a mask, and

you may speak as small as you will.

BOTTOM
An I may hide my face, let me play Thisby too, I'll

speak in a monstrous little voice. 'Thisne,

Thisne;' 'Ah, Pyramus, lover dear! thy Thisby dear,

and lady dear!'

QUINCE
No, no; you must play Pyramus: and, Flute, you Thisby.

BOTTOM
Well, proceed.

QUINCE
Robin Starveling, the tailor.

STARVELING
Here, Peter Quince.

QUINCE
Robin Starveling, you must play Thisby's mother.

Tom Snout, the tinker.

SNOUT
Here, Peter Quince.

QUINCE
You, Pyramus' father: myself, Thisby's father:

Snug, the joiner; you, the lion's part: and, I

hope, here is a play fitted.

SNUG
Have you the lion's part written? pray you, if it

be, give it me, for I am slow of study.

QUINCE
You may do it extempore, for it is nothing but roaring.

BOTTOM
Let me play the lion too: I will roar, that I will

do any man's heart good to hear me; I will roar,

that I will make the duke say 'Let him roar again,

let him roar again.'

QUINCE
An you should do it too terribly, you would fright

the duchess and the ladies, that they would shriek;

and that were enough to hang us all.

ALL
That would hang us, every mother's son.

BOTTOM

I grant you, friends, if that you should fright the

ladies out of their wits, they would have no more

discretion but to hang us: but I will aggravate my

voice so that I will roar you as gently as any

sucking dove; I will roar you an 'twere any

nightingale.

QUINCE

You can play no part but Pyramus; for Pyramus is a

sweet-faced man; a proper man, as one shall see in a

summer's day; a most lovely gentleman-like man:

therefore you must needs play Pyramus.

BOTTOM

Well, I will undertake it. What beard were I best

to play it in?

QUINCE

Why, what you will.

BOTTOM

I will discharge it in either your straw-colour

beard, your orange-tawny beard, your purple-in-grain

beard, or your French-crown-colour beard, your

perfect yellow.

QUINCE

Some of your French crowns have no hair at all, and

then you will play bare-faced. But, masters, here

are your parts: and I am to entreat you, request

you and desire you, to con them by to-morrow night;

and meet me in the palace wood, a mile without the

town, by moonlight; there will we rehearse, for if

we meet in the city, we shall be dogged with

company, and our devices known. In the meantime I

will draw a bill of properties, such as our play

wants. I pray you, fail me not.

BOTTOM
We will meet; and there we may rehearse most

obscenely and courageously. Take pains; be perfect: adieu.

QUINCE
At the duke's oak we meet.

BOTTOM
Enough; hold or cut bow-strings.

Exeunt

NOTES

NOTES

NOTES

ACT II

SCENE I. A wood near Athens.

Enter, from opposite sides, a Fairy, and PUCK

PUCK
How now, spirit! whither wander you?

Fairy
Over hill, over dale,

Thorough bush, thorough brier,

Over park, over pale,

Thorough flood, thorough fire,

I do wander everywhere,

Swifter than the moon's sphere;

And I serve the fairy queen,

To dew her orbs upon the green.

The cowslips tall her pensioners be:

In their gold coats spots you see;

Those be rubies, fairy favours,

In those freckles live their savours:

I must go seek some dewdrops here

And hang a pearl in every cowslip's ear.

Farewell, thou lob of spirits; I'll be gone:

Our queen and all our elves come here anon.

PUCK
The king doth keep his revels here to-night:

Take heed the queen come not within his sight;

For Oberon is passing fell and wrath,

Because that she as her attendant hath

A lovely boy, stolen from an Indian king;

She never had so sweet a changeling;

And jealous Oberon would have the child

Knight of his train, to trace the forests wild;

But she perforce withholds the loved boy,

Crowns him with flowers and makes him all her joy:

And now they never meet in grove or green,

By fountain clear, or spangled starlight sheen,

But, they do square, that all their elves for fear

Creep into acorn-cups and hide them there.

Fairy
Either I mistake your shape and making quite,

Or else you are that shrewd and knavish sprite

Call'd Robin Goodfellow: are not you he

That frights the maidens of the villagery;

Skim milk, and sometimes labour in the quern

And bootless make the breathless housewife churn;

And sometime make the drink to bear no barm;

Mislead night-wanderers, laughing at their harm?

Those that Hobgoblin call you and sweet Puck,

You do their work, and they shall have good luck:

Are not you he?

PUCK
Thou speak'st aright;

I am that merry wanderer of the night.

I jest to Oberon and make him smile

When I a fat and bean-fed horse beguile,

Neighing in likeness of a filly foal:

And sometime lurk I in a gossip's bowl,

In very likeness of a roasted crab,

And when she drinks, against her lips I bob

And on her wither'd dewlap pour the ale.

The wisest aunt, telling the saddest tale,

Sometime for three-foot stool mistaketh me;

Then slip I from her bum, down topples she,

And 'tailor' cries, and falls into a cough;

And then the whole quire hold their hips and laugh,

And waxen in their mirth and neeze and swear

A merrier hour was never wasted there.

But, room, fairy! here comes Oberon.

Fairy
And here my mistress. Would that he were gone!

Enter, from one side, OBERON, with his train; from the other, TITANIA, with hers

OBERON
Ill met by moonlight, proud Titania.

TITANIA
What, jealous Oberon! Fairies, skip hence:

I have forsworn his bed and company.

OBERON
Tarry, rash wanton: am not I thy lord?

TITANIA
Then I must be thy lady: but I know

When thou hast stolen away from fairy land,

And in the shape of Corin sat all day,

Playing on pipes of corn and versing love

To amorous Phillida. Why art thou here,

Come from the farthest Steppe of India?

But that, forsooth, the bouncing Amazon,

Your buskin'd mistress and your warrior love,

To Theseus must be wedded, and you come

To give their bed joy and prosperity.

OBERON
How canst thou thus for shame, Titania,

Glance at my credit with Hippolyta,

Knowing I know thy love to Theseus?

Didst thou not lead him through the glimmering night

From Perigenia, whom he ravished?

And make him with fair AEgle break his faith,

With Ariadne and Antiopa?

TITANIA
These are the forgeries of jealousy:

And never, since the middle summer's spring,

Met we on hill, in dale, forest or mead,

By paved fountain or by rushy brook,

Or in the beached margent of the sea,

To dance our ringlets to the whistling wind,

But with thy brawls thou hast disturb'd our sport.

Therefore the winds, piping to us in vain,

As in revenge, have suck'd up from the sea

Contagious fogs; which falling in the land

Have every pelting river made so proud

That they have overborne their continents:

The ox hath therefore stretch'd his yoke in vain,

The ploughman lost his sweat, and the green corn

Hath rotted ere his youth attain'd a beard;

The fold stands empty in the drowned field,

And crows are fatted with the murrion flock;

The nine men's morris is fill'd up with mud,

And the quaint mazes in the wanton green

For lack of tread are undistinguishable:

The human mortals want their winter here;

No night is now with hymn or carol blest:

Therefore the moon, the governess of floods,

Pale in her anger, washes all the air,

That rheumatic diseases do abound:

And thorough this distemperature we see

The seasons alter: hoary-headed frosts

Far in the fresh lap of the crimson rose,

And on old Hiems' thin and icy crown

An odorous chaplet of sweet summer buds

Is, as in mockery, set: the spring, the summer,

The childing autumn, angry winter, change

Their wonted liveries, and the mazed world,

By their increase, now knows not which is which:

And this same progeny of evils comes

From our debate, from our dissension;

We are their parents and original.

OBERON
Do you amend it then; it lies in you:

Why should Titania cross her Oberon?

I do but beg a little changeling boy,

To be my henchman.

TITANIA
Set your heart at rest:

The fairy land buys not the child of me.

His mother was a votaress of my order:

And, in the spiced Indian air, by night,

Full often hath she gossip'd by my side,

And sat with me on Neptune's yellow sands,

Marking the embarked traders on the flood,

When we have laugh'd to see the sails conceive

And grow big-bellied with the wanton wind;

Which she, with pretty and with swimming gait

Following,--her womb then rich with my young squire,--

Would imitate, and sail upon the land,

To fetch me trifles, and return again,

As from a voyage, rich with merchandise.

But she, being mortal, of that boy did die;

And for her sake do I rear up her boy,

And for her sake I will not part with him.

OBERON
How long within this wood intend you stay?

TITANIA
Perchance till after Theseus' wedding-day.

If you will patiently dance in our round

And see our moonlight revels, go with us;

If not, shun me, and I will spare your haunts.

OBERON
Give me that boy, and I will go with thee.

TITANIA
Not for thy fairy kingdom. Fairies, away!

We shall chide downright, if I longer stay.

Exit TITANIA with her train
OBERON
Well, go thy way: thou shalt not from this grove

Till I torment thee for this injury.

My gentle Puck, come hither. Thou rememberest

Since once I sat upon a promontory,

And heard a mermaid on a dolphin's back

Uttering such dulcet and harmonious breath

That the rude sea grew civil at her song

And certain stars shot madly from their spheres,

To hear the sea-maid's music.

PUCK
I remember.

OBERON
That very time I saw, but thou couldst not,

Flying between the cold moon and the earth,

Cupid all arm'd: a certain aim he took

At a fair vestal throned by the west,

And loosed his love-shaft smartly from his bow,

As it should pierce a hundred thousand hearts;

But I might see young Cupid's fiery shaft

Quench'd in the chaste beams of the watery moon,

And the imperial votaress passed on,

In maiden meditation, fancy-free.

Yet mark'd I where the bolt of Cupid fell:

It fell upon a little western flower,

Before milk-white, now purple with love's wound,

And maidens call it love-in-idleness.

Fetch me that flower; the herb I shew'd thee once:

The juice of it on sleeping eye-lids laid

Will make or man or woman madly dote

Upon the next live creature that it sees.

Fetch me this herb; and be thou here again

Ere the leviathan can swim a league.

PUCK
I'll put a girdle round about the earth

In forty minutes.

Exit
OBERON
Having once this juice,

I'll watch Titania when she is asleep,

And drop the liquor of it in her eyes.

The next thing then she waking looks upon,

Be it on lion, bear, or wolf, or bull,

On meddling monkey, or on busy ape,

She shall pursue it with the soul of love:

And ere I take this charm from off her sight,

As I can take it with another herb,

I'll make her render up her page to me.

But who comes here? I am invisible;

And I will overhear their conference.

Enter DEMETRIUS, HELENA, following him
DEMETRIUS
I love thee not, therefore pursue me not.

Where is Lysander and fair Hermia?

The one I'll slay, the other slayeth me.

Thou told'st me they were stolen unto this wood;

And here am I, and wode within this wood,

Because I cannot meet my Hermia.

Hence, get thee gone, and follow me no more.

HELENA
You draw me, you hard-hearted adamant;

But yet you draw not iron, for my heart

Is true as steel: leave you your power to draw,

And I shall have no power to follow you.

DEMETRIUS
Do I entice you? do I speak you fair?

Or, rather, do I not in plainest truth

Tell you, I do not, nor I cannot love you?

HELENA
And even for that do I love you the more.

I am your spaniel; and, Demetrius,

The more you beat me, I will fawn on you:

Use me but as your spaniel, spurn me, strike me,

Neglect me, lose me; only give me leave,

Unworthy as I am, to follow you.

What worser place can I beg in your love,--

And yet a place of high respect with me,--

Than to be used as you use your dog?

DEMETRIUS
Tempt not too much the hatred of my spirit;

For I am sick when I do look on thee.

HELENA
And I am sick when I look not on you.

DEMETRIUS
You do impeach your modesty too much,

To leave the city and commit yourself

Into the hands of one that loves you not;

To trust the opportunity of night

And the ill counsel of a desert place

With the rich worth of your virginity.

HELENA
Your virtue is my privilege: for that

It is not night when I do see your face,

Therefore I think I am not in the night;

Nor doth this wood lack worlds of company,

For you in my respect are all the world:

Then how can it be said I am alone,

When all the world is here to look on me?

DEMETRIUS
I'll run from thee and hide me in the brakes,

And leave thee to the mercy of wild beasts.

HELENA
The wildest hath not such a heart as you.

Run when you will, the story shall be changed:

Apollo flies, and Daphne holds the chase;

The dove pursues the griffin; the mild hind

Makes speed to catch the tiger; bootless speed,

When cowardice pursues and valour flies.

DEMETRIUS
I will not stay thy questions; let me go:

Or, if thou follow me, do not believe

But I shall do thee mischief in the wood.

HELENA

Ay, in the temple, in the town, the field,

You do me mischief. Fie, Demetrius!

Your wrongs do set a scandal on my sex:

We cannot fight for love, as men may do;

We should be wood and were not made to woo.

Exit DEMETRIUS
I'll follow thee and make a heaven of hell,

To die upon the hand I love so well.

Exit
OBERON

Fare thee well, nymph: ere he do leave this grove,

Thou shalt fly him and he shall seek thy love.

Re-enter PUCK
Hast thou the flower there? Welcome, wanderer.

PUCK

Ay, there it is.

OBERON

I pray thee, give it me.

I know a bank where the wild thyme blows,

Where oxlips and the nodding violet grows,

Quite over-canopied with luscious woodbine,

With sweet musk-roses and with eglantine:

There sleeps Titania sometime of the night,

Lull'd in these flowers with dances and delight;

And there the snake throws her enamell'd skin,

Weed wide enough to wrap a fairy in:

And with the juice of this I'll streak her eyes,

And make her full of hateful fantasies.

Take thou some of it, and seek through this grove:

A sweet Athenian lady is in love

With a disdainful youth: anoint his eyes;

But do it when the next thing he espies

May be the lady: thou shalt know the man

By the Athenian garments he hath on.

Effect it with some care, that he may prove

More fond on her than she upon her love:

And look thou meet me ere the first cock crow.

PUCK
Fear not, my lord, your servant shall do so.

Exeunt

NOTES

SCENE II. Another part of the wood.

Enter TITANIA, with her train

TITANIA
Come, now a roundel and a fairy song;

Then, for the third part of a minute, hence;

Some to kill cankers in the musk-rose buds,

Some war with rere-mice for their leathern wings,

To make my small elves coats, and some keep back

The clamorous owl that nightly hoots and wonders

At our quaint spirits. Sing me now asleep;

Then to your offices and let me rest.

The Fairies sing
You spotted snakes with double tongue,

Thorny hedgehogs, be not seen;

Newts and blind-worms, do no wrong,

Come not near our fairy queen.

Philomel, with melody

Sing in our sweet lullaby;

Lulla, lulla, lullaby, lulla, lulla, lullaby:

Never harm,

Nor spell nor charm,

Come our lovely lady nigh;

So, good night, with lullaby.

Weaving spiders, come not here;

Hence, you long-legg'd spinners, hence!

Beetles black, approach not near;

Worm nor snail, do no offence.

Philomel, with melody, & c.

Fairy
Hence, away! now all is well:

One aloof stand sentinel.

Exeunt Fairies. TITANIA sleeps
Enter OBERON and squeezes the flower on TITANIA's eyelids
OBERON
What thou seest when thou dost wake,

Do it for thy true-love take,

Love and languish for his sake:

Be it ounce, or cat, or bear,

Pard, or boar with bristled hair,

In thy eye that shall appear

When thou wakest, it is thy dear:

Wake when some vile thing is near.

Exit
Enter LYSANDER and HERMIA
LYSANDER
Fair love, you faint with wandering in the wood;

And to speak troth, I have forgot our way:

We'll rest us, Hermia, if you think it good,

And tarry for the comfort of the day.

HERMIA
Be it so, Lysander: find you out a bed;

For I upon this bank will rest my head.

LYSANDER
One turf shall serve as pillow for us both;

One heart, one bed, two bosoms and one troth.

HERMIA
Nay, good Lysander; for my sake, my dear,

Lie further off yet, do not lie so near.

LYSANDER
O, take the sense, sweet, of my innocence!

Love takes the meaning in love's conference.

I mean, that my heart unto yours is knit

So that but one heart we can make of it;

Two bosoms interchained with an oath;

So then two bosoms and a single troth.

Then by your side no bed-room me deny;

For lying so, Hermia, I do not lie.

HERMIA
Lysander riddles very prettily:

Now much beshrew my manners and my pride,

If Hermia meant to say Lysander lied.

But, gentle friend, for love and courtesy

Lie further off; in human modesty,

Such separation as may well be said

Becomes a virtuous bachelor and a maid,

So far be distant; and, good night, sweet friend:

Thy love ne'er alter till thy sweet life end!

LYSANDER
Amen, amen, to that fair prayer, say I;

And then end life when I end loyalty!

Here is my bed: sleep give thee all his rest!

HERMIA
With half that wish the wisher's eyes be press'd!

They sleep
Enter PUCK
PUCK
Through the forest have I gone.

But Athenian found I none,

On whose eyes I might approve

This flower's force in stirring love.

Night and silence.--Who is here?

Weeds of Athens he doth wear:

This is he, my master said,

Despised the Athenian maid;

And here the maiden, sleeping sound,

On the dank and dirty ground.

Pretty soul! she durst not lie

Near this lack-love, this kill-courtesy.

Churl, upon thy eyes I throw

All the power this charm doth owe.

When thou wakest, let love forbid

Sleep his seat on thy eyelid:

So awake when I am gone;

For I must now to Oberon.

Exit
Enter DEMETRIUS and HELENA, running
HELENA
Stay, though thou kill me, sweet Demetrius.

DEMETRIUS
I charge thee, hence, and do not haunt me thus.

HELENA
O, wilt thou darkling leave me? do not so.

DEMETRIUS
Stay, on thy peril: I alone will go.

Exit
HELENA
O, I am out of breath in this fond chase!

The more my prayer, the lesser is my grace.

Happy is Hermia, wheresoe'er she lies;

For she hath blessed and attractive eyes.

How came her eyes so bright? Not with salt tears:

If so, my eyes are oftener wash'd than hers.

No, no, I am as ugly as a bear;

For beasts that meet me run away for fear:

Therefore no marvel though Demetrius

Do, as a monster fly my presence thus.

What wicked and dissembling glass of mine

Made me compare with Hermia's sphery eyne?

But who is here? Lysander! on the ground!

Dead? or asleep? I see no blood, no wound.

Lysander if you live, good sir, awake.

LYSANDER
[Awaking] And run through fire I will for thy sweet sake.

Transparent Helena! Nature shows art,

That through thy bosom makes me see thy heart.

Where is Demetrius? O, how fit a word

Is that vile name to perish on my sword!

HELENA
Do not say so, Lysander; say not so

What though he love your Hermia? Lord, what though?

Yet Hermia still loves you: then be content.

LYSANDER
Content with Hermia! No; I do repent

The tedious minutes I with her have spent.

Not Hermia but Helena I love:

Who will not change a raven for a dove?

The will of man is by his reason sway'd;

And reason says you are the worthier maid.

Things growing are not ripe until their season

So I, being young, till now ripe not to reason;

And touching now the point of human skill,

Reason becomes the marshal to my will

And leads me to your eyes, where I o'erlook

Love's stories written in love's richest book.

HELENA
Wherefore was I to this keen mockery born?

When at your hands did I deserve this scorn?

Is't not enough, is't not enough, young man,

That I did never, no, nor never can,

Deserve a sweet look from Demetrius' eye,

But you must flout my insufficiency?

Good troth, you do me wrong, good sooth, you do,

In such disdainful manner me to woo.

But fare you well: perforce I must confess

I thought you lord of more true gentleness.

O, that a lady, of one man refused.

Should of another therefore be abused!

Exit
LYSANDER
She sees not Hermia. Hermia, sleep thou there:

And never mayst thou come Lysander near!

For as a surfeit of the sweetest things

The deepest loathing to the stomach brings,

Or as tie heresies that men do leave

Are hated most of those they did deceive,

So thou, my surfeit and my heresy,

Of all be hated, but the most of me!

And, all my powers, address your love and might

To honour Helen and to be her knight!

Exit
HERMIA
[Awaking] Help me, Lysander, help me! do thy best

To pluck this crawling serpent from my breast!

Ay me, for pity! what a dream was here!

Lysander, look how I do quake with fear:

Methought a serpent eat my heart away,

And you sat smiling at his cruel pray.

Lysander! what, removed? Lysander! lord!

What, out of hearing? gone? no sound, no word?

Alack, where are you speak, an if you hear;

Speak, of all loves! I swoon almost with fear.

No? then I well perceive you all not nigh

Either death or you I'll find immediately.

Exit

NOTES

NOTES

ACT III

SCENE I. The wood. TITANIA lying asleep.

Enter QUINCE, SNUG, BOTTOM, FLUTE, SNOUT, and STARVELING

BOTTOM
Are we all met?

QUINCE
Pat, pat; and here's a marvellous convenient place

for our rehearsal. This green plot shall be our

stage, this hawthorn-brake our tiring-house; and we

will do it in action as we will do it before the duke.

BOTTOM
Peter Quince,--

QUINCE
What sayest thou, bully Bottom?

BOTTOM
There are things in this comedy of Pyramus and

Thisby that will never please. First, Pyramus must

draw a sword to kill himself; which the ladies

cannot abide. How answer you that?

SNOUT
By'r lakin, a parlous fear.

STARVELING
I believe we must leave the killing out, when all is done.

BOTTOM
Not a whit: I have a device to make all well.

Write me a prologue; and let the prologue seem to

say, we will do no harm with our swords, and that

Pyramus is not killed indeed; and, for the more

better assurance, tell them that I, Pyramus, am not

Pyramus, but Bottom the weaver: this will put them

out of fear.

QUINCE
Well, we will have such a prologue; and it shall be

written in eight and six.

BOTTOM
No, make it two more; let it be written in eight and eight.

SNOUT
Will not the ladies be afeard of the lion?

STARVELING
I fear it, I promise you.

BOTTOM
Masters, you ought to consider with yourselves: to

bring in--God shield us!--a lion among ladies, is a

most dreadful thing; for there is not a more fearful

wild-fowl than your lion living; and we ought to

look to 't.

SNOUT
Therefore another prologue must tell he is not a lion.

BOTTOM
Nay, you must name his name, and half his face must

be seen through the lion's neck: and he himself

must speak through, saying thus, or to the same

defect,--'Ladies,'--or 'Fair-ladies--I would wish

You,'--or 'I would request you,'--or 'I would

entreat you,--not to fear, not to tremble: my life

for yours. If you think I come hither as a lion, it

were pity of my life: no I am no such thing; I am a

man as other men are;' and there indeed let him name

his name, and tell them plainly he is Snug the joiner.

QUINCE
Well it shall be so. But there is two hard things;

that is, to bring the moonlight into a chamber; for,

you know, Pyramus and Thisby meet by moonlight.

SNOUT
Doth the moon shine that night we play our play?

BOTTOM
A calendar, a calendar! look in the almanac; find

out moonshine, find out moonshine.

QUINCE
Yes, it doth shine that night.

BOTTOM
Why, then may you leave a casement of the great

chamber window, where we play, open, and the moon

may shine in at the casement.

QUINCE
Ay; or else one must come in with a bush of thorns

and a lanthorn, and say he comes to disfigure, or to

present, the person of Moonshine. Then, there is

another thing: we must have a wall in the great

chamber; for Pyramus and Thisby says the story, did

talk through the chink of a wall.

SNOUT
You can never bring in a wall. What say you, Bottom?

BOTTOM
Some man or other must present Wall: and let him

have some plaster, or some loam, or some rough-cast

about him, to signify wall; and let him hold his

fingers thus, and through that cranny shall Pyramus

and Thisby whisper.

QUINCE
If that may be, then all is well. Come, sit down,

every mother's son, and rehearse your parts.

Pyramus, you begin: when you have spoken your

speech, enter into that brake: and so every one

according to his cue.

Enter PUCK behind
PUCK
What hempen home-spuns have we swaggering here,

So near the cradle of the fairy queen?

What, a play toward! I'll be an auditor;

An actor too, perhaps, if I see cause.

QUINCE
Speak, Pyramus. Thisby, stand forth.

BOTTOM
Thisby, the flowers of odious savours sweet,--

QUINCE
Odours, odours.

BOTTOM
--odours savours sweet:

So hath thy breath, my dearest Thisby dear.

But hark, a voice! stay thou but here awhile,

And by and by I will to thee appear.

Exit
PUCK
A stranger Pyramus than e'er played here.

Exit
FLUTE
Must I speak now?

QUINCE
Ay, marry, must you; for you must understand he goes

but to see a noise that he heard, and is to come again.

FLUTE
Most radiant Pyramus, most lily-white of hue,

Of colour like the red rose on triumphant brier,

Most brisky juvenal and eke most lovely Jew,

As true as truest horse that yet would never tire,

I'll meet thee, Pyramus, at Ninny's tomb.

QUINCE

'Ninus' tomb,' man: why, you must not speak that

yet; that you answer to Pyramus: you speak all your

part at once, cues and all Pyramus enter: your cue

is past; it is, 'never tire.'

FLUTE

O,--As true as truest horse, that yet would

never tire.

Re-enter PUCK, and BOTTOM with an ass's head
BOTTOM

If I were fair, Thisby, I were only thine.

QUINCE

O monstrous! O strange! we are haunted. Pray,

masters! fly, masters! Help!

Exeunt QUINCE, SNUG, FLUTE, SNOUT, and STARVELING
PUCK

I'll follow you, I'll lead you about a round,

Through bog, through bush, through brake, through brier:

Sometime a horse I'll be, sometime a hound,

A hog, a headless bear, sometime a fire;

And neigh, and bark, and grunt, and roar, and burn,

Like horse, hound, hog, bear, fire, at every turn.

Exit
BOTTOM

Why do they run away? this is a knavery of them to

make me afeard.

Re-enter SNOUT

SNOUT

O Bottom, thou art changed! what do I see on thee?

BOTTOM

What do you see? you see an asshead of your own, do

you?

Exit SNOUT
Re-enter QUINCE
QUINCE

Bless thee, Bottom! bless thee! thou art

translated.

Exit
BOTTOM

I see their knavery: this is to make an ass of me;

to fright me, if they could. But I will not stir

from this place, do what they can: I will walk up

and down here, and I will sing, that they shall hear

I am not afraid.

Sings
The ousel cock so black of hue,

With orange-tawny bill,

The throstle with his note so true,

The wren with little quill,--

TITANIA

[Awaking] What angel wakes me from my flowery bed?

BOTTOM

[Sings]

The finch, the sparrow and the lark,

The plain-song cuckoo gray,

Whose note full many a man doth mark,

And dares not answer nay;--

for, indeed, who would set his wit to so foolish

a bird? who would give a bird the lie, though he cry

'cuckoo' never so?

TITANIA
I pray thee, gentle mortal, sing again:

Mine ear is much enamour'd of thy note;

So is mine eye enthralled to thy shape;

And thy fair virtue's force perforce doth move me

On the first view to say, to swear, I love thee.

BOTTOM
Methinks, mistress, you should have little reason

for that: and yet, to say the truth, reason and

love keep little company together now-a-days; the

more the pity that some honest neighbours will not

make them friends. Nay, I can gleek upon occasion.

TITANIA
Thou art as wise as thou art beautiful.

BOTTOM
Not so, neither: but if I had wit enough to get out

of this wood, I have enough to serve mine own turn.

TITANIA
Out of this wood do not desire to go:

Thou shalt remain here, whether thou wilt or no.

I am a spirit of no common rate;

The summer still doth tend upon my state;

And I do love thee: therefore, go with me;

I'll give thee fairies to attend on thee,

And they shall fetch thee jewels from the deep,

And sing while thou on pressed flowers dost sleep;

And I will purge thy mortal grossness so

That thou shalt like an airy spirit go.

Peaseblossom! Cobweb! Moth! and Mustardseed!

Enter PEASEBLOSSOM, COBWEB, MOTH, and MUSTARDSEED
PEASEBLOSSOM
Ready.

COBWEB
And I.

MOTH
And I.

MUSTARDSEED
And I.

ALL
Where shall we go?

TITANIA
Be kind and courteous to this gentleman;

Hop in his walks and gambol in his eyes;

Feed him with apricocks and dewberries,

With purple grapes, green figs, and mulberries;

The honey-bags steal from the humble-bees,

And for night-tapers crop their waxen thighs

And light them at the fiery glow-worm's eyes,

To have my love to bed and to arise;

And pluck the wings from Painted butterflies

To fan the moonbeams from his sleeping eyes:

Nod to him, elves, and do him courtesies.

PEASEBLOSSOM
Hail, mortal!

COBWEB
Hail!

MOTH
Hail!

MUSTARDSEED
Hail!

BOTTOM
I cry your worship's mercy, heartily: I beseech your

worship's name.

COBWEB
Cobweb.

BOTTOM
I shall desire you of more acquaintance, good Master

Cobweb: if I cut my finger, I shall make bold with

you. Your name, honest gentleman?

PEASEBLOSSOM
Peaseblossom.

BOTTOM
I pray you, commend me to Mistress Squash, your

mother, and to Master Peascod, your father. Good

Master Peaseblossom, I shall desire you of more

acquaintance too. Your name, I beseech you, sir?

MUSTARDSEED
Mustardseed.

BOTTOM
Good Master Mustardseed, I know your patience well:

that same cowardly, giant-like ox-beef hath

devoured many a gentleman of your house: I promise

you your kindred had made my eyes water ere now. I

desire your more acquaintance, good Master

Mustardseed.

TITANIA
Come, wait upon him; lead him to my bower.

The moon methinks looks with a watery eye;

And when she weeps, weeps every little flower,

Lamenting some enforced chastity.

Tie up my love's tongue bring him silently.

Exeunt

SCENE II. Another part of the wood.

Enter OBERON

OBERON
I wonder if Titania be awaked;

Then, what it was that next came in her eye,

Which she must dote on in extremity.

Enter PUCK
Here comes my messenger.

How now, mad spirit!

What night-rule now about this haunted grove?

PUCK
My mistress with a monster is in love.

Near to her close and consecrated bower,

While she was in her dull and sleeping hour,

A crew of patches, rude mechanicals,

That work for bread upon Athenian stalls,

Were met together to rehearse a play

Intended for great Theseus' nuptial-day.

The shallowest thick-skin of that barren sort,

Who Pyramus presented, in their sport

Forsook his scene and enter'd in a brake

When I did him at this advantage take,

An ass's nole I fixed on his head:

Anon his Thisbe must be answered,

And forth my mimic comes. When they him spy,

As wild geese that the creeping fowler eye,

Or russet-pated choughs, many in sort,

Rising and cawing at the gun's report,

Sever themselves and madly sweep the sky,

So, at his sight, away his fellows fly;

And, at our stamp, here o'er and o'er one falls;

He murder cries and help from Athens calls.

Their sense thus weak, lost with their fears

thus strong,

Made senseless things begin to do them wrong;

For briers and thorns at their apparel snatch;

Some sleeves, some hats, from yielders all

things catch.

I led them on in this distracted fear,

And left sweet Pyramus translated there:

When in that moment, so it came to pass,

Titania waked and straightway loved an ass.

OBERON
This falls out better than I could devise.

But hast thou yet latch'd the Athenian's eyes

With the love-juice, as I did bid thee do?

PUCK
I took him sleeping,--that is finish'd too,--

And the Athenian woman by his side:

That, when he waked, of force she must be eyed.

Enter HERMIA and DEMETRIUS
OBERON
Stand close: this is the same Athenian.

PUCK
This is the woman, but not this the man.

DEMETRIUS
O, why rebuke you him that loves you so?

Lay breath so bitter on your bitter foe.

HERMIA
Now I but chide; but I should use thee worse,

For thou, I fear, hast given me cause to curse,

If thou hast slain Lysander in his sleep,

Being o'er shoes in blood, plunge in the deep,

And kill me too.

The sun was not so true unto the day

As he to me: would he have stolen away

From sleeping Hermia? I'll believe as soon

This whole earth may be bored and that the moon

May through the centre creep and so displease

Her brother's noontide with Antipodes.

It cannot be but thou hast murder'd him;

So should a murderer look, so dead, so grim.

DEMETRIUS
So should the murder'd look, and so should I,

Pierced through the heart with your stern cruelty:

Yet you, the murderer, look as bright, as clear,

As yonder Venus in her glimmering sphere.

HERMIA
What's this to my Lysander? where is he?

Ah, good Demetrius, wilt thou give him me?

DEMETRIUS
I had rather give his carcass to my hounds.

HERMIA
Out, dog! out, cur! thou drivest me past the bounds

Of maiden's patience. Hast thou slain him, then?

Henceforth be never number'd among men!

O, once tell true, tell true, even for my sake!

Durst thou have look'd upon him being awake,

And hast thou kill'd him sleeping? O brave touch!

Could not a worm, an adder, do so much?

An adder did it; for with doubler tongue

Than thine, thou serpent, never adder stung.

DEMETRIUS
You spend your passion on a misprised mood:

I am not guilty of Lysander's blood;

Nor is he dead, for aught that I can tell.

HERMIA
I pray thee, tell me then that he is well.

DEMETRIUS
An if I could, what should I get therefore?

HERMIA
A privilege never to see me more.

And from thy hated presence part I so:

See me no more, whether he be dead or no.

Exit
DEMETRIUS
There is no following her in this fierce vein:

Here therefore for a while I will remain.

So sorrow's heaviness doth heavier grow

For debt that bankrupt sleep doth sorrow owe:

Which now in some slight measure it will pay,

If for his tender here I make some stay.

Lies down and sleeps
OBERON
What hast thou done? thou hast mistaken quite

And laid the love-juice on some true-love's sight:

Of thy misprision must perforce ensue

Some true love turn'd and not a false turn'd true.

PUCK
Then fate o'er-rules, that, one man holding troth,

A million fail, confounding oath on oath.

OBERON

About the wood go swifter than the wind,

And Helena of Athens look thou find:

All fancy-sick she is and pale of cheer,

With sighs of love, that costs the fresh blood dear:

By some illusion see thou bring her here:

I'll charm his eyes against she do appear.

PUCK

I go, I go; look how I go,

Swifter than arrow from the Tartar's bow.

Exit

OBERON

Flower of this purple dye,

Hit with Cupid's archery,

Sink in apple of his eye.

When his love he doth espy,

Let her shine as gloriously

As the Venus of the sky.

When thou wakest, if she be by,

Beg of her for remedy.

Re-enter PUCK

PUCK

Captain of our fairy band,

Helena is here at hand;

And the youth, mistook by me,

Pleading for a lover's fee.

Shall we their fond pageant see?

Lord, what fools these mortals be!

OBERON
Stand aside: the noise they make

Will cause Demetrius to awake.

PUCK
Then will two at once woo one;

That must needs be sport alone;

And those things do best please me

That befal preposterously.

Enter LYSANDER and HELENA
LYSANDER
Why should you think that I should woo in scorn?

Scorn and derision never come in tears:

Look, when I vow, I weep; and vows so born,

In their nativity all truth appears.

How can these things in me seem scorn to you,

Bearing the badge of faith, to prove them true?

HELENA
You do advance your cunning more and more.

When truth kills truth, O devilish-holy fray!

These vows are Hermia's: will you give her o'er?

Weigh oath with oath, and you will nothing weigh:

Your vows to her and me, put in two scales,

Will even weigh, and both as light as tales.

LYSANDER
I had no judgment when to her I swore.

HELENA
Nor none, in my mind, now you give her o'er.

LYSANDER
Demetrius loves her, and he loves not you.

DEMETRIUS
[Awaking] O Helena, goddess, nymph, perfect, divine!

To what, my love, shall I compare thine eyne?

Crystal is muddy. O, how ripe in show

Thy lips, those kissing cherries, tempting grow!

That pure congealed white, high Taurus snow,

Fann'd with the eastern wind, turns to a crow

When thou hold'st up thy hand: O, let me kiss

This princess of pure white, this seal of bliss!

HELENA
O spite! O hell! I see you all are bent

To set against me for your merriment:

If you we re civil and knew courtesy,

You would not do me thus much injury.

Can you not hate me, as I know you do,

But you must join in souls to mock me too?

If you were men, as men you are in show,

You would not use a gentle lady so;

To vow, and swear, and superpraise my parts,

When I am sure you hate me with your hearts.

You both are rivals, and love Hermia;

And now both rivals, to mock Helena:

A trim exploit, a manly enterprise,

To conjure tears up in a poor maid's eyes

With your derision! none of noble sort

Would so offend a virgin, and extort

A poor soul's patience, all to make you sport.

LYSANDER
You are unkind, Demetrius; be not so;

For you love Hermia; this you know I know:

And here, with all good will, with all my heart,

In Hermia's love I yield you up my part;

And yours of Helena to me bequeath,

Whom I do love and will do till my death.

HELENA
Never did mockers waste more idle breath.

DEMETRIUS
Lysander, keep thy Hermia; I will none:

If e'er I loved her, all that love is gone.

My heart to her but as guest-wise sojourn'd,

And now to Helen is it home return'd,

There to remain.

LYSANDER
Helen, it is not so.

DEMETRIUS
Disparage not the faith thou dost not know,

Lest, to thy peril, thou aby it dear.

Look, where thy love comes; yonder is thy dear.

Re-enter HERMIA
HERMIA
Dark night, that from the eye his function takes,

The ear more quick of apprehension makes;

Wherein it doth impair the seeing sense,

It pays the hearing double recompense.

Thou art not by mine eye, Lysander, found;

Mine ear, I thank it, brought me to thy sound

But why unkindly didst thou leave me so?

LYSANDER
Why should he stay, whom love doth press to go?

HERMIA
What love could press Lysander from my side?

LYSANDER
Lysander's love, that would not let him bide,

Fair Helena, who more engilds the night

Than all you fiery oes and eyes of light.

Why seek'st thou me? could not this make thee know,

The hate I bear thee made me leave thee so?

HERMIA
You speak not as you think: it cannot be.

HELENA
Lo, she is one of this confederacy!

Now I perceive they have conjoin'd all three

To fashion this false sport, in spite of me.

Injurious Hermia! most ungrateful maid!

Have you conspired, have you with these contrived

To bait me with this foul derision?

Is all the counsel that we two have shared,

The sisters' vows, the hours that we have spent,

When we have chid the hasty-footed time

For parting us,--O, is it all forgot?

All school-days' friendship, childhood innocence?

We, Hermia, like two artificial gods,

Have with our needles created both one flower,

Both on one sampler, sitting on one cushion,

Both warbling of one song, both in one key,

As if our hands, our sides, voices and minds,

Had been incorporate. So we grow together,

Like to a double cherry, seeming parted,

But yet an union in partition;

Two lovely berries moulded on one stem;

So, with two seeming bodies, but one heart;

Two of the first, like coats in heraldry,

Due but to one and crowned with one crest.

And will you rent our ancient love asunder,

To join with men in scorning your poor friend?

It is not friendly, 'tis not maidenly:

Our sex, as well as I, may chide you for it,

Though I alone do feel the injury.

HERMIA
I am amazed at your passionate words.

I scorn you not: it seems that you scorn me.

HELENA
Have you not set Lysander, as in scorn,

To follow me and praise my eyes and face?

And made your other love, Demetrius,

Who even but now did spurn me with his foot,

To call me goddess, nymph, divine and rare,

Precious, celestial? Wherefore speaks he this

To her he hates? and wherefore doth Lysander

Deny your love, so rich within his soul,

And tender me, forsooth, affection,

But by your setting on, by your consent?

What thought I be not so in grace as you,

So hung upon with love, so fortunate,

But miserable most, to love unloved?

This you should pity rather than despise.

HERNIA
I understand not what you mean by this.

HELENA
Ay, do, persever, counterfeit sad looks,

Make mouths upon me when I turn my back;

Wink each at other; hold the sweet jest up:

This sport, well carried, shall be chronicled.

If you have any pity, grace, or manners,

You would not make me such an argument.

But fare ye well: 'tis partly my own fault;

Which death or absence soon shall remedy.

LYSANDER
Stay, gentle Helena; hear my excuse:

My love, my life my soul, fair Helena!

HELENA
O excellent!

HERMIA
Sweet, do not scorn her so.

DEMETRIUS
If she cannot entreat, I can compel.

LYSANDER
Thou canst compel no more than she entreat:

Thy threats have no more strength than her weak prayers.

Helen, I love thee; by my life, I do:

I swear by that which I will lose for thee,

To prove him false that says I love thee not.

DEMETRIUS
I say I love thee more than he can do.

LYSANDER
If thou say so, withdraw, and prove it too.

DEMETRIUS
Quick, come!

HERMIA
Lysander, whereto tends all this?

LYSANDER
Away, you Ethiope!

DEMETRIUS
No, no; he'll [ ]

Seem to break loose; take on as you would follow,

But yet come not: you are a tame man, go!

LYSANDER
Hang off, thou cat, thou burr! vile thing, let loose,

Or I will shake thee from me like a serpent!

HERMIA
Why are you grown so rude? what change is this?

Sweet love,--

LYSANDER
Thy love! out, tawny Tartar, out!

Out, loathed medicine! hated potion, hence!

HERMIA
Do you not jest?

HELENA
Yes, sooth; and so do you.

LYSANDER
Demetrius, I will keep my word with thee.

DEMETRIUS
I would I had your bond, for I perceive

A weak bond holds you: I'll not trust your word.

LYSANDER
What, should I hurt her, strike her, kill her dead?

Although I hate her, I'll not harm her so.

HERMIA
What, can you do me greater harm than hate?

Hate me! wherefore? O me! what news, my love!

Am not I Hermia? are not you Lysander?

I am as fair now as I was erewhile.

Since night you loved me; yet since night you left

me:

Why, then you left me--O, the gods forbid!--

In earnest, shall I say?

LYSANDER
Ay, by my life;

And never did desire to see thee more.

Therefore be out of hope, of question, of doubt;

Be certain, nothing truer; 'tis no jest

That I do hate thee and love Helena.

HERMIA
O me! you juggler! you canker-blossom!

You thief of love! what, have you come by night

And stolen my love's heart from him?

HELENA
Fine, i'faith!

Have you no modesty, no maiden shame,

No touch of bashfulness? What, will you tear

Impatient answers from my gentle tongue?

Fie, fie! you counterfeit, you puppet, you!

HERMIA
Puppet? why so? ay, that way goes the game.

Now I perceive that she hath made compare

Between our statures; she hath urged her height;

And with her personage, her tall personage,

Her height, forsooth, she hath prevail'd with him.

And are you grown so high in his esteem;

Because I am so dwarfish and so low?

How low am I, thou painted maypole? speak;

How low am I? I am not yet so low

But that my nails can reach unto thine eyes.

HELENA
I pray you, though you mock me, gentlemen,

Let her not hurt me: I was never curst;

I have no gift at all in shrewishness;

I am a right maid for my cowardice:

Let her not strike me. You perhaps may think,

Because she is something lower than myself,

That I can match her.

HERMIA
Lower! hark, again.

HELENA
Good Hermia, do not be so bitter with me.

I evermore did love you, Hermia,

Did ever keep your counsels, never wrong'd you;

Save that, in love unto Demetrius,

I told him of your stealth unto this wood.

He follow'd you; for love I follow'd him;

But he hath chid me hence and threaten'd me

To strike me, spurn me, nay, to kill me too:

And now, so you will let me quiet go,

To Athens will I bear my folly back

And follow you no further: let me go:

You see how simple and how fond I am.

HERMIA
Why, get you gone: who is't that hinders you?

HELENA
A foolish heart, that I leave here behind.

HERMIA
What, with Lysander?

HELENA
With Demetrius.

LYSANDER
Be not afraid; she shall not harm thee, Helena.

DEMETRIUS
No, sir, she shall not, though you take her part.

HELENA
O, when she's angry, she is keen and shrewd!

She was a vixen when she went to school;

And though she be but little, she is fierce.

HERMIA
'Little' again! nothing but 'low' and 'little'!

Why will you suffer her to flout me thus?

Let me come to her.

LYSANDER
Get you gone, you dwarf;

You minimus, of hindering knot-grass made;

You bead, you acorn.

DEMETRIUS
You are too officious

In her behalf that scorns your services.

Let her alone: speak not of Helena;

Take not her part; for, if thou dost intend

Never so little show of love to her,

Thou shalt aby it.

LYSANDER
Now she holds me not;

Now follow, if thou darest, to try whose right,

Of thine or mine, is most in Helena.

DEMETRIUS
Follow! nay, I'll go with thee, cheek by jole.

Exeunt LYSANDER and DEMETRIUS
HERMIA
You, mistress, all this coil is 'long of you:

Nay, go not back.

HELENA
I will not trust you, I,

Nor longer stay in your curst company.

Your hands than mine are quicker for a fray,

My legs are longer though, to run away.

Exit
HERMIA
I am amazed, and know not what to say.

Exit

OBERON
This is thy negligence: still thou mistakest,

Or else committ'st thy knaveries wilfully.

PUCK
Believe me, king of shadows, I mistook.

Did not you tell me I should know the man

By the Athenian garment be had on?

And so far blameless proves my enterprise,

That I have 'nointed an Athenian's eyes;

And so far am I glad it so did sort

As this their jangling I esteem a sport.

OBERON
Thou see'st these lovers seek a place to fight:

Hie therefore, Robin, overcast the night;

The starry welkin cover thou anon

With drooping fog as black as Acheron,

And lead these testy rivals so astray

As one come not within another's way.

Like to Lysander sometime frame thy tongue,

Then stir Demetrius up with bitter wrong;

And sometime rail thou like Demetrius;

And from each other look thou lead them thus,

Till o'er their brows death-counterfeiting sleep

With leaden legs and batty wings doth creep:

Then crush this herb into Lysander's eye;

Whose liquor hath this virtuous property,

To take from thence all error with his might,

And make his eyeballs roll with wonted sight.

When they next wake, all this derision

Shall seem a dream and fruitless vision,

And back to Athens shall the lovers wend,

With league whose date till death shall never end.

Whiles I in this affair do thee employ,

I'll to my queen and beg her Indian boy;

And then I will her charmed eye release

From monster's view, and all things shall be peace.

PUCK
My fairy lord, this must be done with haste,

For night's swift dragons cut the clouds full fast,

And yonder shines Aurora's harbinger;

At whose approach, ghosts, wandering here and there,

Troop home to churchyards: damned spirits all,

That in crossways and floods have burial,

Already to their wormy beds are gone;

For fear lest day should look their shames upon,

They willfully themselves exile from light

And must for aye consort with black-brow'd night.

OBERON
But we are spirits of another sort:

I with the morning's love have oft made sport,

And, like a forester, the groves may tread,

Even till the eastern gate, all fiery-red,

Opening on Neptune with fair blessed beams,

Turns into yellow gold his salt green streams.

But, notwithstanding, haste; make no delay:

We may effect this business yet ere day.

Exit
PUCK
Up and down, up and down,

I will lead them up and down:

I am fear'd in field and town:

Goblin, lead them up and down.

Here comes one.

Re-enter LYSANDER
LYSANDER
Where art thou, proud Demetrius? speak thou now.

PUCK
Here, villain; drawn and ready. Where art thou?

LYSANDER
I will be with thee straight.

PUCK
Follow me, then,

To plainer ground.

Exit LYSANDER, as following the voice
Re-enter DEMETRIUS
DEMETRIUS
Lysander! speak again:

Thou runaway, thou coward, art thou fled?

Speak! In some bush? Where dost thou hide thy head?

PUCK
Thou coward, art thou bragging to the stars,

Telling the bushes that thou look'st for wars,

And wilt not come? Come, recreant; come, thou child;

I'll whip thee with a rod: he is defiled

That draws a sword on thee.

DEMETRIUS
Yea, art thou there?

PUCK
Follow my voice: we'll try no manhood here.

Exeunt
Re-enter LYSANDER
LYSANDER
He goes before me and still dares me on:

When I come where he calls, then he is gone.

The villain is much lighter-heel'd than I:

I follow'd fast, but faster he did fly;

That fallen am I in dark uneven way,

And here will rest me.

Lies down

Come, thou gentle day!

For if but once thou show me thy grey light,

I'll find Demetrius and revenge this spite.

Sleeps
Re-enter PUCK and DEMETRIUS
PUCK
Ho, ho, ho! Coward, why comest thou not?

DEMETRIUS
Abide me, if thou darest; for well I wot

Thou runn'st before me, shifting every place,

And darest not stand, nor look me in the face.

Where art thou now?

PUCK
Come hither: I am here.

DEMETRIUS
Nay, then, thou mock'st me. Thou shalt buy this dear,

If ever I thy face by daylight see:

Now, go thy way. Faintness constraineth me

To measure out my length on this cold bed.

By day's approach look to be visited.

Lies down and sleeps

Re-enter HELENA
HELENA
O weary night, O long and tedious night,

Abate thy hour! Shine comforts from the east,

That I may back to Athens by daylight,

From these that my poor company detest:

And sleep, that sometimes shuts up sorrow's eye,

Steal me awhile from mine own company.

Lies down and sleeps

PUCK
Yet but three? Come one more;

Two of both kinds make up four.

Here she comes, curst and sad:

Cupid is a knavish lad,

Thus to make poor females mad.

Re-enter HERMIA
HERMIA
Never so weary, never so in woe,

Bedabbled with the dew and torn with briers,

I can no further crawl, no further go;

My legs can keep no pace with my desires.

Here will I rest me till the break of day.

Heavens shield Lysander, if they mean a fray!

Lies down and sleeps
PUCK
On the ground

Sleep sound:

I'll apply

To your eye,

Gentle lover, remedy.

Squeezing the juice on LYSANDER's eyes

When thou wakest,

Thou takest

True delight

In the sight

Of thy former lady's eye:

And the country proverb known,

That every man should take his own,

In your waking shall be shown:

Jack shall have Jill;

Nought shall go ill;

The man shall have his mare again, and all shall be well.

Exit

NOTES

NOTES

ACT IV

SCENE I. The same. LYSANDER, DEMETRIUS, HELENA, and

HERMIAlying asleep.

Enter TITANIA and BOTTOM; PEASEBLOSSOM, COBWEB, MOTH,
MUSTARDSEED, and other Fairies attending; OBERON behind
unseen

TITANIA
Come, sit thee down upon this flowery bed,

While I thy amiable cheeks do coy,

And stick musk-roses in thy sleek smooth head,

And kiss thy fair large ears, my gentle joy.

BOTTOM
Where's Peaseblossom?

PEASEBLOSSOM
Ready.

BOTTOM
Scratch my head Peaseblossom. Where's Mounsieur Cobweb?

COBWEB
Ready.

BOTTOM
Mounsieur Cobweb, good mounsieur, get you your

weapons in your hand, and kill me a red-hipped

humble-bee on the top of a thistle; and, good

mounsieur, bring me the honey-bag. Do not fret

yourself too much in the action, mounsieur; and,

good mounsieur, have a care the honey-bag break not;

I would be loath to have you overflown with a

honey-bag, signior. Where's Mounsieur Mustardseed?

MUSTARDSEED
Ready.

BOTTOM
Give me your neaf, Mounsieur Mustardseed. Pray you,

leave your courtesy, good mounsieur.

MUSTARDSEED
What's your Will?

BOTTOM
Nothing, good mounsieur, but to help Cavalery Cobweb

to scratch. I must to the barber's, monsieur; for

methinks I am marvellous hairy about the face; and I

am such a tender ass, if my hair do but tickle me,

I must scratch.

TITANIA
What, wilt thou hear some music,

my sweet love?

BOTTOM
I have a reasonable good ear in music. Let's have

the tongs and the bones.

TITANIA
Or say, sweet love, what thou desirest to eat.

BOTTOM
Truly, a peck of provender: I could munch your good

dry oats. Methinks I have a great desire to a bottle

of hay: good hay, sweet hay, hath no fellow.

TITANIA
I have a venturous fairy that shall seek

The squirrel's hoard, and fetch thee new nuts.

BOTTOM
I had rather have a handful or two of dried peas.

But, I pray you, let none of your people stir me: I

have an exposition of sleep come upon me.

TITANIA
Sleep thou, and I will wind thee in my arms.

Fairies, begone, and be all ways away.

Exeunt fairies

So doth the woodbine the sweet honeysuckle

Gently entwist; the female ivy so

Enrings the barky fingers of the elm.

O, how I love thee! how I dote on thee!

They sleep
Enter PUCK
OBERON
[Advancing] Welcome, good Robin.

See'st thou this sweet sight?

Her dotage now I do begin to pity:

For, meeting her of late behind the wood,

Seeking sweet favours from this hateful fool,

I did upbraid her and fall out with her;

For she his hairy temples then had rounded

With a coronet of fresh and fragrant flowers;

And that same dew, which sometime on the buds

Was wont to swell like round and orient pearls,

Stood now within the pretty flowerets' eyes

Like tears that did their own disgrace bewail.

When I had at my pleasure taunted her

And she in mild terms begg'd my patience,

I then did ask of her her changeling child;

Which straight she gave me, and her fairy sent

To bear him to my bower in fairy land.

And now I have the boy, I will undo

This hateful imperfection of her eyes:

And, gentle Puck, take this transformed scalp

From off the head of this Athenian swain;

That, he awaking when the other do,

May all to Athens back again repair

And think no more of this night's accidents

But as the fierce vexation of a dream.

But first I will release the fairy queen.

Be as thou wast wont to be;

See as thou wast wont to see:

Dian's bud o'er Cupid's flower

Hath such force and blessed power.

Now, my Titania; wake you, my sweet queen.

TITANIA
My Oberon! what visions have I seen!

Methought I was enamour'd of an ass.

OBERON
There lies your love.

TITANIA
How came these things to pass?

O, how mine eyes do loathe his visage now!

OBERON
Silence awhile. Robin, take off this head.

Titania, music call; and strike more dead

Than common sleep of all these five the sense.

TITANIA
Music, ho! music, such as charmeth sleep!

Music, still
PUCK
Now, when thou wakest, with thine

own fool's eyes peep.

OBERON
Sound, music! Come, my queen, take hands with me,

And rock the ground whereon these sleepers be.

Now thou and I are new in amity,

And will to-morrow midnight solemnly

Dance in Duke Theseus' house triumphantly,

And bless it to all fair prosperity:

There shall the pairs of faithful lovers be

Wedded, with Theseus, all in jollity.

PUCK
Fairy king, attend, and mark:

I do hear the morning lark.

OBERON
Then, my queen, in silence sad,

Trip we after the night's shade:

We the globe can compass soon,

Swifter than the wandering moon.

TITANIA
Come, my lord, and in our flight

Tell me how it came this night

That I sleeping here was found

With these mortals on the ground.

Exeunt
Horns winded within
Enter THESEUS, HIPPOLYTA, EGEUS, and train

THESEUS
Go, one of you, find out the forester;

For now our observation is perform'd;

And since we have the vaward of the day,

My love shall hear the music of my hounds.

Uncouple in the western valley; let them go:

Dispatch, I say, and find the forester.

Exit an Attendant

We will, fair queen, up to the mountain's top,

And mark the musical confusion

Of hounds and echo in conjunction.

HIPPOLYTA
I was with Hercules and Cadmus once,

When in a wood of Crete they bay'd the bear

With hounds of Sparta: never did I hear

Such gallant chiding: for, besides the groves,

The skies, the fountains, every region near

Seem'd all one mutual cry: I never heard

So musical a discord, such sweet thunder.

THESEUS
My hounds are bred out of the Spartan kind,

So flew'd, so sanded, and their heads are hung

With ears that sweep away the morning dew;

Crook-knee'd, and dew-lapp'd like Thessalian bulls;

Slow in pursuit, but match'd in mouth like bells,

Each under each. A cry more tuneable

Was never holla'd to, nor cheer'd with horn,

In Crete, in Sparta, nor in Thessaly:

Judge when you hear. But, soft! what nymphs are these?

EGEUS
My lord, this is my daughter here asleep;

And this, Lysander; this Demetrius is;

This Helena, old Nedar's Helena:

I wonder of their being here together.

THESEUS
No doubt they rose up early to observe

The rite of May, and hearing our intent,

Came here in grace our solemnity.

But speak, Egeus; is not this the day

That Hermia should give answer of her choice?

EGEUS
It is, my lord.

THESEUS
Go, bid the huntsmen wake them with their horns.

Horns and shout within. LYSANDER, DEMETRIUS, HELENA, and

HERMIA wake and start up

Good morrow, friends. Saint Valentine is past:

Begin these wood-birds but to couple now?

LYSANDER
Pardon, my lord.

THESEUS
I pray you all, stand up.

I know you two are rival enemies:

How comes this gentle concord in the world,

That hatred is so far from jealousy,

To sleep by hate, and fear no enmity?

LYSANDER
My lord, I shall reply amazedly,

Half sleep, half waking: but as yet, I swear,

I cannot truly say how I came here;

But, as I think,--for truly would I speak,

And now do I bethink me, so it is,--

I came with Hermia hither: our intent

Was to be gone from Athens, where we might,

Without the peril of the Athenian law.

EGEUS
Enough, enough, my lord; you have enough:

I beg the law, the law, upon his head.

They would have stolen away; they would, Demetrius,

Thereby to have defeated you and me,

You of your wife and me of my consent,

Of my consent that she should be your wife.

DEMETRIUS
My lord, fair Helen told me of their stealth,

Of this their purpose hither to this wood;

And I in fury hither follow'd them,

Fair Helena in fancy following me.

But, my good lord, I wot not by what power,--

But by some power it is,--my love to Hermia,

Melted as the snow, seems to me now

As the remembrance of an idle gaud

Which in my childhood I did dote upon;

And all the faith, the virtue of my heart,

The object and the pleasure of mine eye,

Is only Helena. To her, my lord,

Was I betroth'd ere I saw Hermia:

But, like in sickness, did I loathe this food;

But, as in health, come to my natural taste,

Now I do wish it, love it, long for it,

And will for evermore be true to it.

THESEUS
Fair lovers, you are fortunately met:

Of this discourse we more will hear anon.

Egeus, I will overbear your will;

For in the temple by and by with us

These couples shall eternally be knit:

And, for the morning now is something worn,

Our purposed hunting shall be set aside.

Away with us to Athens; three and three,

We'll hold a feast in great solemnity.

Come, Hippolyta.

Exeunt THESEUS, HIPPOLYTA, EGEUS, and train
DEMETRIUS
These things seem small and undistinguishable,

HERMIA
Methinks I see these things with parted eye,

When every thing seems double.

HELENA
So methinks:

And I have found Demetrius like a jewel,

Mine own, and not mine own.

DEMETRIUS
Are you sure

That we are awake? It seems to me

That yet we sleep, we dream. Do not you think

The duke was here, and bid us follow him?

HERMIA
Yea; and my father.

HELENA
And Hippolyta.

LYSANDER
And he did bid us follow to the temple.

DEMETRIUS
Why, then, we are awake: let's follow him

And by the way let us recount our dreams.

Exeunt

BOTTOM

[Awaking] When my cue comes, call me, and I will

answer: my next is, 'Most fair Pyramus.' Heigh-ho!

Peter Quince! Flute, the bellows-mender! Snout,

the tinker! Starveling! God's my life, stolen

hence, and left me asleep! I have had a most rare

vision. I have had a dream, past the wit of man to

say what dream it was: man is but an ass, if he go

about to expound this dream. Methought I was--there

is no man can tell what. Methought I was,--and

methought I had,--but man is but a patched fool, if

he will offer to say what methought I had. The eye

of man hath not heard, the ear of man hath not

seen, man's hand is not able to taste, his tongue

to conceive, nor his heart to report, what my dream

was. I will get Peter Quince to write a ballad of

this dream: it shall be called Bottom's Dream,

because it hath no bottom; and I will sing it in the

latter end of a play, before the duke:

peradventure, to make it the more gracious, I shall

sing it at her death.

Exit

NOTES

SCENE II. Athens. QUINCE'S house.

Enter QUINCE, FLUTE, SNOUT, and STARVELING

QUINCE
Have you sent to Bottom's house ? is he come home yet?

STARVELING
He cannot be heard of. Out of doubt he is

transported.

FLUTE
If he come not, then the play is marred: it goes

not forward, doth it?

QUINCE
It is not possible: you have not a man in all

Athens able to discharge Pyramus but he.

FLUTE
No, he hath simply the best wit of any handicraft

man in Athens.

QUINCE
Yea and the best person too; and he is a very

paramour for a sweet voice.

FLUTE
You must say 'paragon:' a paramour is, God bless us,

a thing of naught.

Enter SNUG
SNUG
Masters, the duke is coming from the temple, and

there is two or three lords and ladies more married:

if our sport had gone forward, we had all been made

men.

FLUTE
O sweet bully Bottom! Thus hath he lost sixpence a

day during his life; he could not have 'scaped

sixpence a day: an the duke had not given him

sixpence a day for playing Pyramus, I'll be hanged;

he would have deserved it: sixpence a day in

Pyramus, or nothing.

Enter BOTTOM
BOTTOM
Where are these lads? where are these hearts?

QUINCE
Bottom! O most courageous day! O most happy hour!

BOTTOM
Masters, I am to discourse wonders: but ask me not

what; for if I tell you, I am no true Athenian. I

will tell you every thing, right as it fell out.

QUINCE
Let us hear, sweet Bottom.

BOTTOM
Not a word of me. All that I will tell you is, that

the duke hath dined. Get your apparel together,

good strings to your beards, new ribbons to your

pumps; meet presently at the palace; every man look

o'er his part; for the short and the long is, our

play is preferred. In any case, let Thisby have

clean linen; and let not him that plays the lion

pair his nails, for they shall hang out for the

lion's claws. And, most dear actors, eat no onions

nor garlic, for we are to utter sweet breath; and I

do not doubt but to hear them say, it is a sweet

comedy. No more words: away! go, away!

Exeunt

NOTES

NOTES

ACT V

SCENE I. Athens. The palace of THESEUS.

Enter THESEUS, HIPPOLYTA, PHILOSTRATE, Lords and Attendants

HIPPOLYTA
'Tis strange my Theseus, that these

lovers speak of.

THESEUS
More strange than true: I never may believe

These antique fables, nor these fairy toys.

Lovers and madmen have such seething brains,

Such shaping fantasies, that apprehend

More than cool reason ever comprehends.

The lunatic, the lover and the poet

Are of imagination all compact:

One sees more devils than vast hell can hold,

That is, the madman: the lover, all as frantic,

Sees Helen's beauty in a brow of Egypt:

The poet's eye, in fine frenzy rolling,

Doth glance from heaven to earth, from earth to heaven;

And as imagination bodies forth

The forms of things unknown, the poet's pen

Turns them to shapes and gives to airy nothing

A local habitation and a name.

Such tricks hath strong imagination,

That if it would but apprehend some joy,

It comprehends some bringer of that joy;

Or in the night, imagining some fear,

How easy is a bush supposed a bear!

HIPPOLYTA
But all the story of the night told over,

And all their minds transfigured so together,

More witnesseth than fancy's images

And grows to something of great constancy;

But, howsoever, strange and admirable.

THESEUS
Here come the lovers, full of joy and mirth.

Enter LYSANDER, DEMETRIUS, HERMIA, and HELENA
Joy, gentle friends! joy and fresh days of love

Accompany your hearts!

LYSANDER
More than to us

Wait in your royal walks, your board, your bed!

THESEUS
Come now; what masques, what dances shall we have,

To wear away this long age of three hours

Between our after-supper and bed-time?

Where is our usual manager of mirth?

What revels are in hand? Is there no play,

To ease the anguish of a torturing hour?

Call Philostrate.

PHILOSTRATE
Here, mighty Theseus.

THESEUS
Say, what abridgement have you for this evening?

What masque? what music? How shall we beguile

The lazy time, if not with some delight?

PHILOSTRATE
There is a brief how many sports are ripe:

Make choice of which your highness will see first.

Giving a paper
THESEUS
[Reads] 'The battle with the Centaurs, to be sung

By an Athenian eunuch to the harp.'

We'll none of that: that have I told my love,

In glory of my kinsman Hercules.

Reads
'The riot of the tipsy Bacchanals,

Tearing the Thracian singer in their rage.'

That is an old device; and it was play'd

When I from Thebes came last a conqueror.

Reads
'The thrice three Muses mourning for the death

Of Learning, late deceased in beggary.'

That is some satire, keen and critical,

Not sorting with a nuptial ceremony.

Reads

'A tedious brief scene of young Pyramus

And his love Thisbe; very tragical mirth.'

Merry and tragical! tedious and brief!

That is, hot ice and wondrous strange snow.

How shall we find the concord of this discord?

PHILOSTRATE
A play there is, my lord, some ten words long,

Which is as brief as I have known a play;

But by ten words, my lord, it is too long,

Which makes it tedious; for in all the play

There is not one word apt, one player fitted:

And tragical, my noble lord, it is;

For Pyramus therein doth kill himself.

Which, when I saw rehearsed, I must confess,

Made mine eyes water; but more merry tears

The passion of loud laughter never shed.

THESEUS
What are they that do play it?

PHILOSTRATE
Hard-handed men that work in Athens here,

Which never labour'd in their minds till now,

And now have toil'd their unbreathed memories

With this same play, against your nuptial.

THESEUS
And we will hear it.

PHILOSTRATE
No, my noble lord;

It is not for you: I have heard it over,

And it is nothing, nothing in the world;

Unless you can find sport in their intents,

Extremely stretch'd and conn'd with cruel pain,

To do you service.

THESEUS
I will hear that play;

For never anything can be amiss,

When simpleness and duty tender it.

Go, bring them in: and take your places, ladies.

Exit PHILOSTRATE
HIPPOLYTA
I love not to see wretchedness o'er charged

And duty in his service perishing.

THESEUS
Why, gentle sweet, you shall see no such thing.

HIPPOLYTA
He says they can do nothing in this kind.

THESEUS
The kinder we, to give them thanks for nothing.

Our sport shall be to take what they mistake:

And what poor duty cannot do, noble respect

Takes it in might, not merit.

Where I have come, great clerks have purposed

To greet me with premeditated welcomes;

Where I have seen them shiver and look pale,

Make periods in the midst of sentences,

Throttle their practised accent in their fears

And in conclusion dumbly have broke off,

Not paying me a welcome. Trust me, sweet,

Out of this silence yet I pick'd a welcome;

And in the modesty of fearful duty

I read as much as from the rattling tongue

Of saucy and audacious eloquence.

Love, therefore, and tongue-tied simplicity

In least speak most, to my capacity.

Re-enter PHILOSTRATE
PHILOSTRATE
So please your grace, the Prologue is address'd.
THESEUS

Let him approach.

Flourish of trumpets
Enter QUINCE for the Prologue

Prologue

If we offend, it is with our good will.

That you should think, we come not to offend,

But with good will. To show our simple skill,

That is the true beginning of our end.

Consider then we come but in despite.

We do not come as minding to contest you,

Our true intent is. All for your delight

We are not here. That you should here repent you,

The actors are at hand and by their show

You shall know all that you are like to know.

THESEUS
This fellow doth not stand upon points.

LYSANDER
He hath rid his prologue like a rough colt; he knows

not the stop. A good moral, my lord: it is not

enough to speak, but to speak true.

HIPPOLYTA
Indeed he hath played on his prologue like a child

on a recorder; a sound, but not in government.

THESEUS
His speech, was like a tangled chain; nothing

impaired, but all disordered. Who is next?

Enter Pyramus and Thisbe, Wall, Moonshine, and Lion

Prologue

Gentles, perchance you wonder at this show;

But wonder on, till truth make all things plain.

This man is Pyramus, if you would know;

This beauteous lady Thisby is certain.

This man, with lime and rough-cast, doth present

Wall, that vile Wall which did these lovers sunder;

And through Wall's chink, poor souls, they are content

To whisper. At the which let no man wonder.

This man, with lanthorn, dog, and bush of thorn,

Presenteth Moonshine; for, if you will know,

By moonshine did these lovers think no scorn

To meet at Ninus' tomb, there, there to woo.

This grisly beast, which Lion hight by name,

The trusty Thisby, coming first by night,

Did scare away, or rather did affright;

And, as she fled, her mantle she did fall,

Which Lion vile with bloody mouth did stain.

Anon comes Pyramus, sweet youth and tall,

And finds his trusty Thisby's mantle slain:

Whereat, with blade, with bloody blameful blade,

He bravely broach'd is boiling bloody breast;

And Thisby, tarrying in mulberry shade,

His dagger drew, and died. For all the rest,

Let Lion, Moonshine, Wall, and lovers twain

At large discourse, while here they do remain.

Exeunt Prologue, Thisbe, Lion, and Moonshine

THESEUS
I wonder if the lion be to speak.

DEMETRIUS
No wonder, my lord: one lion may, when many asses do.

Wall
In this same interlude it doth befall

That I, one Snout by name, present a wall;

And such a wall, as I would have you think,

That had in it a crannied hole or chink,

Through which the lovers, Pyramus and Thisby,

Did whisper often very secretly.

This loam, this rough-cast and this stone doth show

That I am that same wall; the truth is so:

And this the cranny is, right and sinister,

Through which the fearful lovers are to whisper.

THESEUS
Would you desire lime and hair to speak better?

DEMETRIUS
It is the wittiest partition that ever I heard

discourse, my lord.

Enter Pyramus

THESEUS
Pyramus draws near the wall: silence!

Pyramus
O grim-look'd night! O night with hue so black!

O night, which ever art when day is not!

O night, O night! alack, alack, alack,

I fear my Thisby's promise is forgot!

And thou, O wall, O sweet, O lovely wall,

That stand'st between her father's ground and mine!

Thou wall, O wall, O sweet and lovely wall,

Show me thy chink, to blink through with mine eyne!

Wall holds up his fingers

Thanks, courteous wall: Jove shield thee well for this!

But what see I? No Thisby do I see.

O wicked wall, through whom I see no bliss!

Cursed be thy stones for thus deceiving me!

THESEUS
The wall, methinks, being sensible, should curse again.

Pyramus
No, in truth, sir, he should not. 'Deceiving me'

is Thisby's cue: she is to enter now, and I am to

spy her through the wall. You shall see, it will

fall pat as I told you. Yonder she comes.

Enter Thisbe

Thisbe

O wall, full often hast thou heard my moans,

For parting my fair Pyramus and me!

My cherry lips have often kiss'd thy stones,

Thy stones with lime and hair knit up in thee.

Pyramus

I see a voice: now will I to the chink,

To spy an I can hear my Thisby's face. Thisby!

Thisbe

My love thou art, my love I think.

Pyramus

Think what thou wilt, I am thy lover's grace;

And, like Limander, am I trusty still.

Thisbe

And I like Helen, till the Fates me kill.

Pyramus

Not Shafalus to Procrus was so true.

Thisbe

As Shafalus to Procrus, I to you.

Pyramus

O kiss me through the hole of this vile wall!

Thisbe

I kiss the wall's hole, not your lips at all.

Pyramus

Wilt thou at Ninny's tomb meet me straightway?

Thisbe

'Tide life, 'tide death, I come without delay.

Exeunt Pyramus and Thisbe

Wall
Thus have I, Wall, my part discharged so;

And, being done, thus Wall away doth go.

Exit
THESEUS
Now is the mural down between the two neighbours.

DEMETRIUS
No remedy, my lord, when walls are so wilful to hear

without warning.

HIPPOLYTA
This is the silliest stuff that ever I heard.

THESEUS
The best in this kind are but shadows; and the worst

are no worse, if imagination amend them.

HIPPOLYTA
It must be your imagination then, and not theirs.

THESEUS
If we imagine no worse of them than they of

themselves, they may pass for excellent men. Here

come two noble beasts in, a man and a lion.

Enter Lion and Moonshine
Lion
You, ladies, you, whose gentle hearts do fear

The smallest monstrous mouse that creeps on floor,

May now perchance both quake and tremble here,

When lion rough in wildest rage doth roar.

Then know that I, one Snug the joiner, am

A lion-fell, nor else no lion's dam;

For, if I should as lion come in strife

Into this place, 'twere pity on my life.

THESEUS
A very gentle beast, of a good conscience.

DEMETRIUS
The very best at a beast, my lord, that e'er I saw.

LYSANDER
This lion is a very fox for his valour.

THESEUS
True; and a goose for his discretion.

DEMETRIUS
Not so, my lord; for his valour cannot carry his

discretion; and the fox carries the goose.

THESEUS
His discretion, I am sure, cannot carry his valour;

for the goose carries not the fox. It is well:

leave it to his discretion, and let us listen to the moon.

Moonshine
This lanthorn doth the horned moon present;--

DEMETRIUS
He should have worn the horns on his head.

THESEUS
He is no crescent, and his horns are

invisible within the circumference.

Moonshine

This lanthorn doth the horned moon present;

Myself the man i' the moon do seem to be.

THESEUS

This is the greatest error of all the rest: the man

should be put into the lanthorn. How is it else the

man i' the moon?

DEMETRIUS

He dares not come there for the candle; for, you

see, it is already in snuff.

HIPPOLYTA

I am aweary of this moon: would he would change!

THESEUS

It appears, by his small light of discretion, that

he is in the wane; but yet, in courtesy, in all

reason, we must stay the time.

LYSANDER

Proceed, Moon.

Moonshine

All that I have to say, is, to tell you that the

lanthorn is the moon; I, the man in the moon; this

thorn-bush, my thorn-bush; and this dog, my dog.

DEMETRIUS

Why, all these should be in the lanthorn; for all

these are in the moon. But, silence! here comes Thisbe.

Enter Thisbe

Thisbe
This is old Ninny's tomb. Where is my love?

Lion
[Roaring] Oh--

Thisbe runs off
DEMETRIUS
Well roared, Lion.

THESEUS
Well run, Thisbe.

HIPPOLYTA
Well shone, Moon. Truly, the moon shines with a

good grace.

The Lion shakes Thisbe's mantle, and exit

THESEUS
Well moused, Lion.

LYSANDER
And so the lion vanished.

DEMETRIUS
And then came Pyramus.

Enter Pyramus
Pyramus
Sweet Moon, I thank thee for thy sunny beams;

I thank thee, Moon, for shining now so bright;

For, by thy gracious, golden, glittering gleams,

I trust to take of truest Thisby sight.

But stay, O spite!

But mark, poor knight,

What dreadful dole is here!

Eyes, do you see?

How can it be?

O dainty duck! O dear!

Thy mantle good,

What, stain'd with blood!

Approach, ye Furies fell!

O Fates, come, come,

Cut thread and thrum;

Quail, crush, conclude, and quell!

THESEUS
This passion, and the death of a dear friend, would

go near to make a man look sad.

HIPPOLYTA
Beshrew my heart, but I pity the man.

Pyramus
O wherefore, Nature, didst thou lions frame?

Since lion vile hath here deflower'd my dear:

Which is--no, no--which was the fairest dame

That lived, that loved, that liked, that look'd

with cheer.

Come, tears, confound;

Out, sword, and wound

The pap of Pyramus;

Ay, that left pap,

Where heart doth hop:

Stabs himself

Thus die I, thus, thus, thus.

Now am I dead,

Now am I fled;

My soul is in the sky:

Tongue, lose thy light;

Moon take thy flight:

Exit Moonshine

Now die, die, die, die, die.

Dies

DEMETRIUS
No die, but an ace, for him; for he is but one.

LYSANDER
Less than an ace, man; for he is dead; he is nothing.

THESEUS
With the help of a surgeon he might yet recover, and

prove an ass.

HIPPOLYTA
How chance Moonshine is gone before Thisbe comes

back and finds her lover?

THESEUS
She will find him by starlight. Here she comes; and

her passion ends the play.

Re-enter Thisbe

HIPPOLYTA
Methinks she should not use a long one for such a

Pyramus: I hope she will be brief.

DEMETRIUS
A mote will turn the balance, which Pyramus, which

Thisbe, is the better; he for a man, God warrant us;

she for a woman, God bless us.

LYSANDER
She hath spied him already with those sweet eyes.

DEMETRIUS
And thus she means, videlicet:--

Thisbe
Asleep, my love?

What, dead, my dove?

O Pyramus, arise!

Speak, speak. Quite dumb?

Dead, dead? A tomb

Must cover thy sweet eyes.

These My lips,

This cherry nose,

These yellow cowslip cheeks,

Are gone, are gone:

Lovers, make moan:

His eyes were green as leeks.

O Sisters Three,

Come, come to me,

With hands as pale as milk;

Lay them in gore,

Since you have shore

With shears his thread of silk.

Tongue, not a word:

Come, trusty sword;

Come, blade, my breast imbrue:

Stabs herself

And, farewell, friends;

Thus Thisby ends:

Adieu, adieu, adieu.

Dies
THESEUS
Moonshine and Lion are left to bury the dead.

DEMETRIUS
Ay, and Wall too.

BOTTOM
[Starting up] No assure you; the wall is down that

parted their fathers. Will it please you to see the

epilogue, or to hear a Bergomask dance between two

of our company?

THESEUS
No epilogue, I pray you; for your play needs no

excuse. Never excuse; for when the players are all

dead, there needs none to be blamed. Marry, if he

that writ it had played Pyramus and hanged himself

in Thisbe's garter, it would have been a fine

tragedy: and so it is, truly; and very notably

discharged. But come, your Bergomask: let your

epilogue alone.

A dance
The iron tongue of midnight hath told twelve:

Lovers, to bed; 'tis almost fairy time.

I fear we shall out-sleep the coming morn

As much as we this night have overwatch'd.

This palpable-gross play hath well beguiled

The heavy gait of night. Sweet friends, to bed.

A fortnight hold we this solemnity,

In nightly revels and new jollity.

Exeunt
Enter PUCK
PUCK
Now the hungry lion roars,

And the wolf behowls the moon;

Whilst the heavy ploughman snores,

All with weary task fordone.

Now the wasted brands do glow,

Whilst the screech-owl, screeching loud,

Puts the wretch that lies in woe

In remembrance of a shroud.

Now it is the time of night

That the graves all gaping wide,

Every one lets forth his sprite,

In the church-way paths to glide:

And we fairies, that do run

By the triple Hecate's team,

From the presence of the sun,

Following darkness like a dream,

Now are frolic: not a mouse

Shall disturb this hallow'd house:

I am sent with broom before,

To sweep the dust behind the door.

Enter OBERON and TITANIA with their train
OBERON
Through the house give gathering light,

By the dead and drowsy fire:

Every elf and fairy sprite

Hop as light as bird from brier;

And this ditty, after me,

Sing, and dance it trippingly.

TITANIA
First, rehearse your song by rote

To each word a warbling note:

Hand in hand, with fairy grace,

Will we sing, and bless this place.

Song and dance

OBERON
Now, until the break of day,

Through this house each fairy stray.

To the best bride-bed will we,

Which by us shall blessed be;

And the issue there create

Ever shall be fortunate.

So shall all the couples three

Ever true in loving be;

And the blots of Nature's hand

Shall not in their issue stand;

Never mole, hare lip, nor scar,

Nor mark prodigious, such as are

Despised in nativity,

Shall upon their children be.

With this field-dew consecrate,

Every fairy take his gait;

And each several chamber bless,

Through this palace, with sweet peace;

And the owner of it blest

Ever shall in safety rest.

Trip away; make no stay;

Meet me all by break of day.

Exeunt OBERON, TITANIA, and train
PUCK
If we shadows have offended,

Think but this, and all is mended,

That you have but slumber'd here

While these visions did appear.

And this weak and idle theme,

No more yielding but a dream,

Gentles, do not reprehend:

if you pardon, we will mend:

And, as I am an honest Puck,

If we have unearned luck

Now to 'scape the serpent's tongue,

We will make amends ere long;

Else the Puck a liar call;

So, good night unto you all.

Give me your hands, if we be friends,

And Robin shall restore amends.

NOTES

NOTES

Printed in Great Britain
by Amazon